The Angel
of the
Lost and Found

1980's/90's & 2005

or

Irish Poems

by Peter Isacké

Price £8.50

Published by
Wedderburn Art Ltd
on behalf of Peter Isacké

ISBN 1 905037 06 6

© Peter Isacké

Cover Illustration by Paul Amphlet

Printed by
Impressions of Monmouth Limited
Tel: 01594 839407

Contents

BUTTERFLY SONG AT COOLE

"May I come here?" sang butterfly,
in sultry summer day,
"May I come here and feed on sweet flower", I'd say.
When silent swans are silking,
birds are singing so,
can I come among wild flowers, grasses, Oh!
to hear waves lapping among stones;
to find blue beetle, lazy drone;
water insects busy in season's surprise;
Ladybird flying in breakwing disguise;
bottle green elder-fly, noisy stare …
to hear fairy's horn in soft air
coming from magic, stillness of park
unreal, yet mysterious, dreamlike, stark!
Still can I come, may I come to fair Lakeland fun?
Can I come here?' sang butterfly in splendid array,
"Can I come here, dance among goose stones", I'd say,
with haunting water rippling, leaves rustling so,
can I fly into sunshine, pollen, Oh!
to see wild orchid, hear singing finch,
can I settle on one hallowed, sacred inch?"

(Gort, Galway, Eire, 1980's)

IRISH BY BELL AND CANDLE

Irish by candle, bell, candle,
Bell, candle, as ghost wolves howl!

Melody, by friendly 'how are yer?'
Raised finger, twinkling tale!
Lazy, by gate post, sun, gate post
Idle throat slakes!

Irish, by stony field, fuchsia,
Nun, purple red fuchsia, name:
Irish by ruin, fire, ruin
Passionate hatred the same!

Kneeling, by silent mass, candle,
Priest, confession,
Church, strong guidance …
Hail Mary, holy water are they!

Pray for me sweet Jesus, me sweet Jesus,
Say a prayer for your servant the same!
Irish by bell, candle, name!

By Padraig, Teresa, Shaun, Ellen,
McQuin, Gallager, Linnane, McGloughlin:
By seven brothers, five sisters,
Peasant, peat fire the same!

Whiskey by porter, drinking, laughter,
By song, ballad, fiddling tune!
Irish by drunken, red eyed, fighting,
Drunken, slow stumbling gait!

Irish by Angelus bell, candle,
Prayer, moonlight, flame!
Irish by bell, candle, always!

Ireland, 1980's

HORN HEAD

Up near Bloody Foreland, further from Stag Rocks,
At sunrise, beyond sodden morning,
Standing out clear against headland
Where strongest of waves dash against
Quartzite façade, there rises,
Out of mists, gale, rising rain,
The huge Horn Head!
Like a land god locked for punishment
In heavy stone
Whose literal roar would shake the earth,
Is one hundred million years old,
Pagan, slow, blind,
His hour flourished when Plesiosaurs
Swam through tossing sea,
Primeval fell creatures cried into dawn
With throaty call from mocking night …
Demons of air, mist,
Screaming as the vast rock reared
High above ocean into violent vision …
It was the ferocious Horn Head!

Ireland, 1980's

THE CURREAVAH (Striped or Brindled Moor)

Beyond Elysium, in reaches of outer space
There is a strip of barren land,
It lies above Reason …
On days when cries are heard in the forest
There happens a race of ages!
A thunder is heard of mighty creatures
On the planes at a distance from Paradise,
A stamping of two powerful beasts hurtling over land –
As of potent horses sprinting;
A black one is a Druid's mount,
White is some stony gods
Who is lost now in obscurity of time!
It occurs on this solitary plane,
Steeds, eyes fixed on eternity
Swiftly move over 'striped or brindled moor!'
Sometimes sable horse wins,
In his golden eyes glow's splendour of victory,
Other times ivory coloured overcomes,
In his blue, noble orbs,
Shines recognition of his feat!

Nearby, on this moorland stands a huge man,
Who shouts aloud at end of every contest,
"Halloa, halloa, it is The Correavah!"

Correavah Hotel, Co. Galway, 14/05/85.

SPIDDALL CHAPEL, JUNE 16th 1986

Chapel, lychgate, walled up –
Protestant church, hatred had closed building!
Graveyard kept by local convent;
John Francis, 1776, an inscription read,
Catholic had taken over,
God's ground had not been sacred
For history's sake!

(Eire)

SPRING, IRELAND POEM

I have come in youth of middle age
To walk on beaches the sun caresses,
When saffron shells ring in scented air,
Seen hills grow with golden gorse,
Magic of sapphire loch caught in flash of camera,
Seen vernal flowers, heard cuckoo,
Wondered at all this charm!

(County Clare, 1986)

ABBEY OF THORNS

A little before Bally Vaughn,
Between Hillock of Bray, Mountain of Breathe
Is ruined temple of Kill!
Stretches into North wind
Within sight of cruel Atlantic;
On Winter days apparitions call from The Burren –
Rocky mass, Mulk built
Before 'roaring god' was slain …
It is ruined Abbey of Thorns
That once held council for clouds themselves!
A place of worship for Thorns!
Would stand in their glory,
Like members of the Klu-Klux-Clan
Singing hollow chants!
Kilfield! At Kilfield? Someone asked.
A sacred pasture lies near ancient stones,
When Angelus Bell rings;
(Here in melodious Ireland,)
Tuskbell rings just once
Telling Pikes time of
Silent worship is upon them!

(County Clare, Eire, 1986)

ERIGAL

Erigal, can you call the great Horn Head?
Erigal, however, tall, towering spread,
Erigal, mountain wall, lost, cloud wed.
Erigal, highland call, alone, feared,
Erigal, rising Saul, eternal lost seer ...
Mountain of enchantment, sleep!

(Donegal, Eire, 7ᵗʰ July, 1986)

ANGER

A large pool of tadpoles,
Sun shone, pond dries up!
A man who knew pond stocked with tadpoles
Returns, finds puddle,
One tadpole remaining!
Goes home to get jar
Tired, so lies down for fifteen minutes.
When revisits pool thirty minutes later
Finds crow standing there.
Flies off, when he gets to
Shallowness, tadpole gone.
Even waterbeetle has been eaten!
Very angry vows
Should like to shoot crow!
Thinks Nature very cruel
Other tadpoles having been eaten
Or dried to death by sun!

(Dekreiter, Conemarra, 1986, Eire)

BALLYGANNER CASTLE IN RINGFORT
(gothic description)

Down river Suck
Whose eyeballs cling to waterweed
As if gouged from sheep skulls,
Down 'hobnailed' mountain, where leprechauns spit,
By wedge tomb where 'Tulsk' rooted towers,
Near ancient 'forge of gullet'
Stands bare ruin!
Hands on blue skyline as lark sings,
There are desolate fractures in vaulted arch
As drear phantoms rear terrible heads in gloom!
On 'rhinoceros' nights hollow screams heard by gushing swell.
Near Corofin, where angels rise
Lies Ballyganner Castle in Ringfort!
If God paid me I wouldn't go there
Til lepers laugh dried in yellow throat,
Or under witches kiss, burnt!
Wretched spirits haunt bare walls,
Thunder throbs under lost echo,
Even trees are dead!
Last place Spring rises –
Ballyganner Castle in Ringfort!

(Gort, Galway, Eire, 1986)

SAINTHOOD AND SUN

Lying near Saint Coleman in summer sun ...
Touch his grave – power of healing felt!
Suns power roasting,
Which is turning,
One wholeness, other scorches!

(Kilmacdugh graveyard, near Gort,
Co. Galway, Eire, 6th July, 1987)

LOCH THOUGHTS

Grey today, reflects sky.
Distant traffic passes likes whispers,
Plane hums above as Godly spinning top,
Daisies grow around moss coloured boulder,
Wind gets up over lake;
Lark sings, Cuckoo calls –
Like walking on vast sponge
Across moorland of Connemara
After much rain – how it poured!
Parts of bog too soft to walk on,
Must tread carefully!
Return to loch –
How water laps lip and shore!

(Dekrieter, Connemara,
30th May, 1986)

LORD MUSTARD II

We all know Lord Mustard
'Cowardly, cowardly, custard' –
Goes around in filth,
Coughing, spluttering, making mellow,
Belching, bragging, blurting around –
A clown in town!
His huge American radio,
Sulphured flavoured suit –
Better if mute!
Blue jeans, smelly socks,
Best of prattling cocks,
Scarecrows around streets of Galway
Looking for children to eat!
Yarns, tripe, a noisy life
For Alistair, disc jockey, alias Lord Mustard
Staring all zany buffoonery at peoples' weaknesses –
Large Falstaffian man,
Half cockney / Cumbrian accent,
Says he comes from Dundee –
Get yourself home then!

(Galway, Eire, 1988)

14

DONKEY PUDDING (Nonsense Poem)

Donkey, 'ponkey' wonkey pie
Can you 'he-haw' in sky.
Talking donkey, donkey-tea
Swimming in 'Donkey Sea'.

Had 'Monkey Stew',
Followed by Donkey poo
Able to climb trees after,
Bray exceedingly well!

Donkey ducking in pond,
Hippopotamus very fond
Toucans sing, seahorses sigh,
Zebras crossing in sky.

Camel laughing, Lamas cough,
Coat of Elephant very rough!
Reindeer prances, Ostrich strides,
Giraffes find it difficult to hide!

(Ireland, 1988)

DONKEYS

Standing on sandy beach
Watching children riding donkeys
Led by gawky school girls –
Blue sky above gives desolation!

Play together in herd;
Biting, rubbing necks,
Excellent mother with young –
Constantly caressing heads: affectionate!

(Dekrieter, Connemara, Eire, 1988)

CONNEMARRA BOG

Has it always been like this?
Dark soggy peat, green slime, water –
Wet rocks, dead heather, grey-white skeletal wood
Preserved by thick, deep, semi-liquid turf!
Weather whistling in from Atlantic –
Rain, rain, rain, grey cloudy days, glorious sun!
Get dirty on a bog, healthy, away from man,
Timeless, slow,
Ooze, sinking – part of fun!
Shrill call of pewit,
Occasional heron flying over loch!
Wild flowers, stones, thin air,
Insects of every shape; flies, moths,
Especially coleopterous insects!
Sheep, foxes – you never see –
Donkey call, spring turf, clover,
Spikes of marsh grass, bilberries, lichen –
Whites, yellows, creams;
Bleached brown pools where waterbeetles swim –
Ridges, bumps of soft earth – squash, squash, squelch,
Bog frogs, saturation!
Yes it has always been like this!

(Dekreiter, Galway, 1988)

16

TURF CUTTER BUILDS A FIRE
(dedicated to John O' Sullivan)

Here raising
As if playing musical instrument!
Professional! Handles fuel
Moving bits about,
"Neater fire, better ignites." he says,
"Materials bit wet!
Put it by heat to dry!"
Gently prods, fingers,
Even damp peat begins to smoulder!
Flames grow in strength, brightly lit,
Getting warm on wild October night!
Craftsman with blaze,
Touching, building for fifteen minutes
As heat strengthens, glows!
Cuts turf for a living,
Eight children to feed,
Has to know how to construct a fire!

(Dekreiter, Ireland, 1989)

SHEEP DEAD

Bog like sheeps graveyard!
Bones, skulls, horns,
Strewn all over it!
Don't send sheep to abattoir
Die on Natures 'finest' marsh!
One dead this morning
With half arse eaten away!
Stomach bloated, eyes fixed, legs limp, twisted!
Fox, wild cat, by peat shed
Has had feed of her!

Weather changes day by day,
Wild wet weather – calm, quiet,
Dull, drizzle, sun, breeze; storms!
Changes rapidly from Atlantic!

Tiny toadstools grow on manure;
Mushrooms appear, native white ponies frolic,
Donkeys laugh – so it seems!
Face can stay a healthy pink,
No pollution, water is clear!

(Dekreiter, Conemarra, Eire,
18 September 1988)

MUSHROOMS

Coming up like snowdrops, small lambs,
Unaware of danger above earth!
Fungoid cells form in dark soil –
Up they pop innocent as goldfish,
Soon kicked by sheep, bullocks, gathered, or vandalised
Until clean, white, globular heads no more!
Had watched growth overnight
Begin to form into specimens!
Having mushrooms grow by doorstep
Silently charming, quietly magical!
Seeing gentle edible umbrella creatures
Appear together,
Ate two – peeled – fried alive –
Only four left!
Small balls, vulnerable, like Daddy Longlegs,
Cannot help one from spawning
Like caterpillars, tadpoles, will be destroyed
So soft, unprotected they are!

(Dekreiter, Conemarra, Galway,
September 1989

CREEPER

Huge 'witch-hand' creeper
Nearly choked the Ash to death
Until was severed!
Firm wooden tentacles,
Parasitic, sap sucking claws
Piteously strangled form!
Much dead timber
So chopping of climbing plant
May have come too late!

(Dekreiter, September 1989)

A LADY

Came to me
Bearing ivy leaves, arrows;
Wore long black dress and
In her eyes fondness did seem!
Came out of sun
Appearing like a vision!
Wondered if she could be
Fairy or gentle waif!

It was a lady: she was gracious, free;
Talked of calling, bearing fruit,
Also of sadness –
Unsure of ladies name,
Now she's gone from me
With ivy leaves and arrows!

(Gort, Ireland, 1988)

ANGEL OF THE LOST AND FOUND

Tell me boys, come pale and will,
Tell me where you walk?
For 'bride of wing' is carried so
On wooden staves she goes!

Tell me boys, come tell me, what angelic host
Has brought flowers, brought wings
To setting by the sea?
Is it hallowed land you walk on,
Hallowed land and free?

Tell me boys, Oh tell me
As you walk your wintered way
Where misted hills are beyond moorland?
Where water is your play?

What is little angels name?
Why she is blindfolded so?
Blooms she carries too, tell me
Are they symbols of the few?

Yes boys, may I ask
Is this mysterious landscape home?
Is peat bog for sacred,
Is this a child of snow who roams?

/cont.

Why do you look forsaken
Are you walking to the moon?
Is delicate child a spirit
Who died from some consumptive gloom?
Is her name Anya?

What's tree behind you,
A shrub of healing truth?
Does Saint Anya lead you
To blessed freedom beyond blue?

I cannot tell!

(Ireland, 1989)

TERECIA MCGLOUGLIN

I know you, would like to!
Your dark curly hair, comely smile.
Terecia McGlouglin! Sweet strong voice
Among fiddles, by choice, I'd know you!
Clear eyes, sixteen years old,
Natural rhythm as you walk through fields,
Love of nature, your beauty, I'd know you!

(Ennis, Eire, 1989)

SCREAMING AT GLENSTALL ABBEY

At monastery for reflection, meditation,
Sign asks guests to 'Maintain Silence'!
So surprised to hear uncontrolled sobbing, hysterical laugher;
A school at abbey, boy upset perhaps!
Went on in prayerful silence,
Crying out in God given air!
"Under control!" said monk in corridor,
"No need to be concerned!"

Was woman guest with nervous problems
Crying out instead of praying!
I wondered, for instance, if I were
Guest in mental hospital
So different mournful cry
From controlled chanting of monks!
Nurse from school was fetched.
Asked woman what matter was.
"It wasn't me!" she answered.
She was confused!
"Said, it wasn't her." Said nurse.
"Oh it was!" said gentle old man. Friend of disturbed!
"Does she suffer with nerves?" asked monk.
"She does!" he said.

(Limerick Eire, September 1991)

RUIN! THE LAND AROUND NORRIE HENCHY, CO. CLARE

No one living around here,
Even blackberries taste dead!
Cottages deserted, empty,
Church too, staring shell,
Mansion House abandoned, open to skies –
Death reigns in gothic intensity!
'Norrie Henchy' roams around with lantern and axe!
Place of isolation, harrowing region of silence, fear!
Pub only opens in evenings,
Locked boarded up all day!

Ever been to Norrie Henchy at night?
Atmosphere of destruction reigns...
Murder near Spancil Hill for the English!

(Written near Ennis, 1991. 'Spancil Hill' very near Norrie Henchy features in an Irish folk song)

ROUNDSTONE HARBOUR

Large dead prey littering bottom on sand;
Small sharks, Sting Ray, two feet long,
Other corpses everywhere – fishes graveyard!
Cruel men have thrown them away
Without thinking of lives ... fishermen!
Ignorant mankind who earn living hunting!
Fish, twisted, still, gills open, white, unpleasant,
Casually thrown away!

(Connemara coast, Galway, August 1991)

24

DEKREITER

Sitting in bungalow on bog
So far from people, (seems so),
You listen, wonder what different noises are;
Hum from electric water pump,
Tick from electric clock,
Wind, bird call, little else!
Sensitivity listens for humans,
Interprets noises, sometimes aren't cars.
When one comes whole silent bog changes!
Place here rather drab, poor, basic;
No carpet on kitchen floor,
Curtains are made of cheap, unattractive material!
Rather haunting, threatening,
As if murder was performed in this solitary place,
Like "presence" still revisited here!

(Connemara, Galway, August, 1991)

TRAGEDY AT GLENGOLA

I remember, sweet, gentle boy
Cycling back from Oughterard, with lovely smile, wave,
As I passed in car.
Or on 'The Commonidge', in July,
Laughing cheerily in firelight, with brother Martin!
Or perhaps it was tucked in corner, playing his fiddle,
Entertaining people in The Boat Inn, Oughterard!
I saw you yesterday sitting in Mother's thatched cottage,
At 21, blonde hair having fallen out,
Leg amputated after malignant growth!
Your Mother explained; months of painful treatment
Before they cut your leg off!
No wonder, you look ill, Dennis Gaughin,
Though still smiling, cheerful,
Eyes bright though you have artificial leg!

(Dekrieter, August 1991)

TREFIN

Oak is growing fishes limbs
Into the air –
Fungus, woody 'flesh' waving!
Do you know Turbot Tarn tumbling with twig-tiddlers?
Have you seen Sapling Salmon
Swimming through timber?
Sycamore Silver Fish are abundant!
Pine Perch I saw;
Hawthorn Hake gulping fresh ether!
Cherry blossom Cod blooming;
Related to Rainbow Trout!
Poplar Plaice, Elm Eels, Mulberry Mackerels,
Ash crabs, Birch Bream – list endless!
All live at Trefin!

(Dekreiter, September, 1991)

CLEGGERT

Is aged Irish witch
Who sits in paper shop all day smoking!
Has a leathery brown face, filmy eyes,
Always seems depressed!
Likes to scowl, get drunk!
Doesn't belong to anybody –
Who'd want her?

(Eire, August, 1991)

STORM IN HEAVEN

Noise of violence flows over hills
Into waterfall which turns violet!

Mountains mumble about missionaries,
Wish with biblical feet
Climb chanting holy presence under rocks!

Bats scream in paradise!
Their images are being burnt –
Turn white into angels ...

Huge, ragged Mounties ride horses into rivers,
Galloping in pursuit of the rich!

Moles ghost digging into clouds,
Building misty homes –
Badgers fly towards sunset.

Mermaids moan under Moon,
While little ghosts blow trumpets!

Mutton men are singing on butcher's shelf
About being sliced into chops, steaks ...
Are blue, juicy, have black eyes.

Sausages spinning under grill –
Breakfast future awaits 'noble poet'!

(Eire, 1991)